little & LARGE
sticker activity book

KNIGHTS & CASTLES

Miles Kelly
PUBLISHING

First published in 2004 by Miles Kelly Publishing Ltd
Bardfield Centre, Great Bardfield, Essex, CM7 4SL

Copyright © Miles Kelly Publishing Ltd 2004

This edition printed in 2008

4 6 8 10 9 7 5 3

Editorial Director: Belinda Gallagher

Art Director: Jo Brewer

Project Manager: Lisa Clayden

Designer: Louisa Leitao

Reprographics: Stephan Davis, Ian Paulyn

Production Manager: Elizabeth Brunwin

British Library Cataloguing-in-Publication Data
A catalogue record for this book is available from the British Library

ISBN 978-1-84236-255-6

Printed in China

All photographs and artworks are from MKP archives

www.mileskelly.net
info@mileskelly.net

www.factsforprojects.com

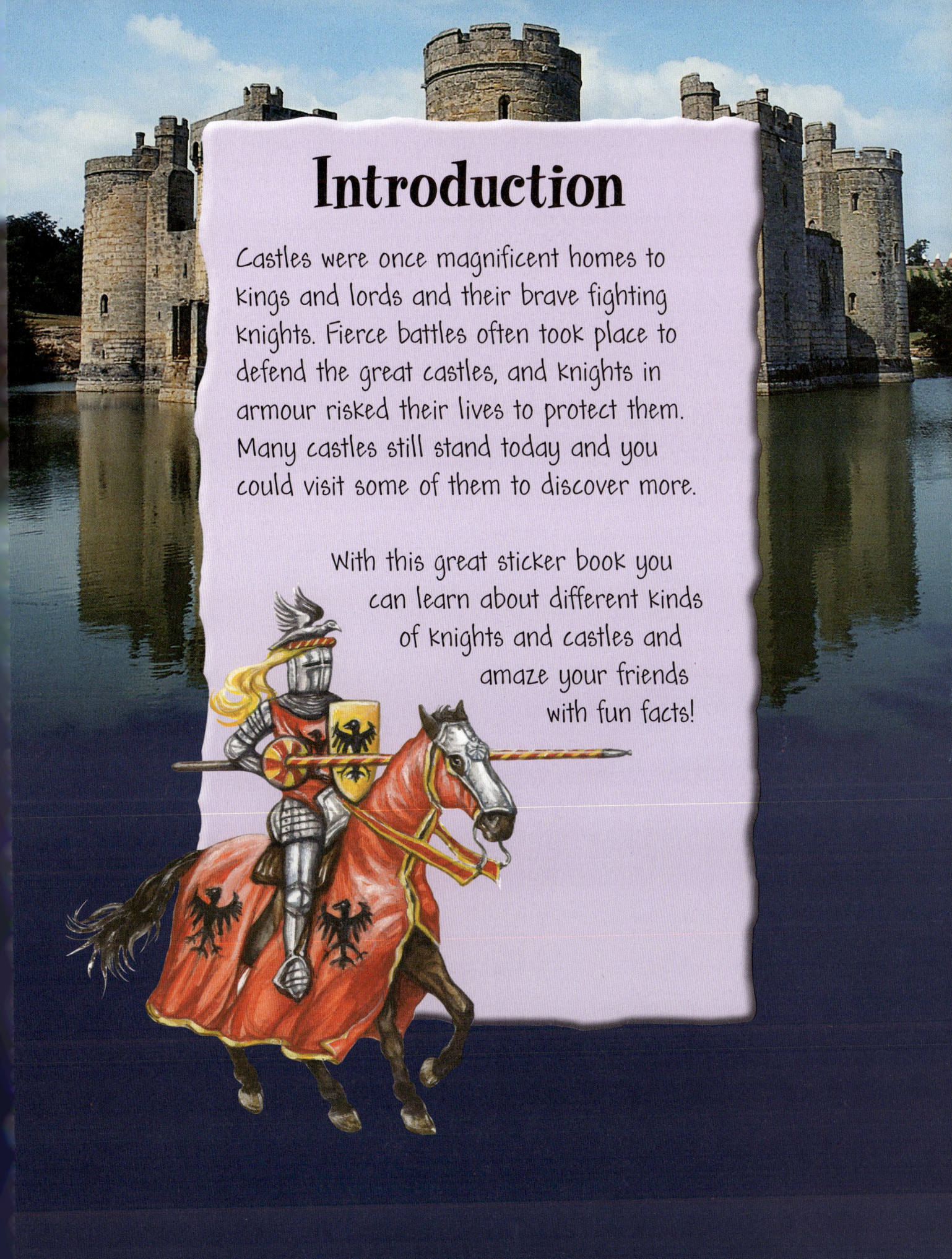

Introduction

Castles were once magnificent homes to kings and lords and their brave fighting knights. Fierce battles often took place to defend the great castles, and knights in armour risked their lives to protect them. Many castles still stand today and you could visit some of them to discover more.

With this great sticker book you can learn about different kinds of knights and castles and amaze your friends with fun facts!

Mini stickers!

What weapons did knights use in battle and at tournaments? Why were castles so cold? What was the code of chivalry? Use your mini stickers to learn all about castles and the knights who defended them.

Knights – skilled soldiers who rode into battle on horseback

Castles – large buildings with towers and battlements, used as fortresses

Weapons – items such as swords and crossbows used at tournaments and in battle

Banners/Shields – used by knights to proudly display their colours and emblems

Knights

▲ Warrior Knight

▲ Knight in armour

▲ Foot combat

▲ Knight and lady

▲ Plate armour

▲ Saracen Knight

▲ Knight and warhorse

▲ Horseback fight

▲ Knight ready for battle

▲ Jousting Knight

▲ English Knight

▲ Knight of St John

▲ Fighting Knights

Castles

▲ Neuschwanstein Castle

▲ Motte and bailey castle

▲ Windsor Castle

▲ Glamis Castle

▲ Castle gate

▲ Berkeley Castle

▲ Early Japanese castle

▲ Conwy Castle

▲ Bodiam Castle

Weapons

▲ Crossbow

▲ Mace

▲ Trebuchet

▲ Sword

▲ Longbow

Banners/Shields

▲ Banner

▲ Knight's shield

▲ Battle shield

▲ Shield

▲ Knight's flag

Knights and castles

◄ Conwy Castle
English monarch Edward I built this castle in Wales between 1283 and 1289

► English Knight
This English Knight is ready to fight for the honour of his country

▲ Knight's flag
Flags showed the knight's colours and coat of arms

▲ Trebuchet
This massive rock-hurling weapon was used to attack castles

▲ Knight's shield
Decorated shields were used by knights as protection during battle

◄ Sword
A sharp double-edged blade was used in battle and during tournament fights

▲ Jousting Knight
In a jousting competition knights carried a shield and lance

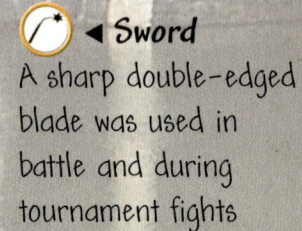

▲ Foot combat
This was a fight between two knights at a tournament

KEY:

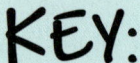

 Knights

 Castles

 Weapons

 Banners/Shields

▶ Berkeley Castle
Built between 1117 and 1153, this castle is said to be haunted by the ghost of Edward II

▲ Saracen knight
These skilled Muslim archers fought in the crusades – religious wars during the Middle Ages

▼ Castle gate
Castle gates often had a heavy grate, called a portcullis, to provide an extra defence barrier

▲ Early Japanese castle
By the 1500s the Japanese were building strong castles

◀ Plate armour
By the 1400s, plate armour covered the knight's whole body

▼ Knight ready for battle
This knight is in full battle armour, carrying his sword and shield

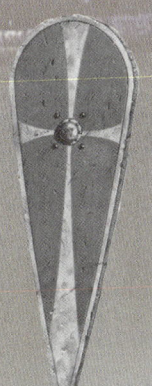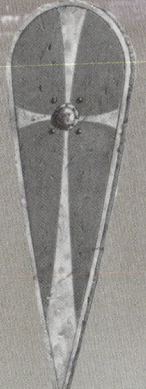

▲ Neuschwanstein Castle
King Ludwig of Bavaria started building this fairytale castle in 1869

▲ Battle shield
A tall, narrow shield used in battle

Some knights cheated in jousts by fixing their armour onto the horse's saddle!

Preparing for battle

Special tournaments were held for knights to help them prepare for proper battles. In a tournament, knights took part in an event called jousting. This involved knights charging at each other at top speed on their horses. The aim was to knock your opponent off his horse with a blow from a long wooden lance.

The knights were protected by armour and they also wore their own personal colours and carried shields. Competing in jousts also gave a knight the chance to prove himself in front of the woman he loved. Jousts were popular events, watched by ladies of the court as well as ordinary people.

The knights held a decorated shield for extra protection

A knight's horse wore matching colours

The wall or tilt helped keep the horses charging in a straight line

▲ Knight's flag

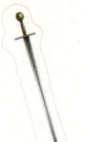

▲ Sword

▲ Conwy Castle

▲ English Knight

▲ Knight's shield

▲ Jousting Knight

▲ Foot combat

▲ Trebuchet

Knights and castles

▲ Knight's flag

▼ Sword

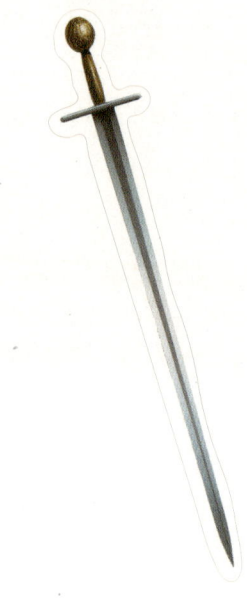

▲ Conwy Castle

▲ English knight

◄ Jousting Knight

▲ Knight's shield

▲ Foot combat

▲ Trebuchet

▲ Neuschwanstein Castle

▲ Saracen Knight

▲ Battle shield

▲ Berkeley Castle

▲ Knight ready
for battle

▲ Early Japanese castle

▲ Plate armour

▲ Castle gate

Knights and castles

▲ Neuschwanstein Castle

▶ Saracen Knight

▲ Berkeley Castle

▲ Battle shield

▶ Knight ready
for battle

▲ Early Japanese
castle

▲ Plate armour

▲ Castle gate

▲ Knight of St John

▲ Knight in armour

▲ Horseback fight

▲ Crossbow

► Mace

▲ Bodiam Castle

▼ Motte and bailey castle

▲ Fighting knights

▲ Knight of St John

▲ Knight in armour

▲ Horseback fight

▲ Crossbow

▲ Bodiam Castle

▲ Mace

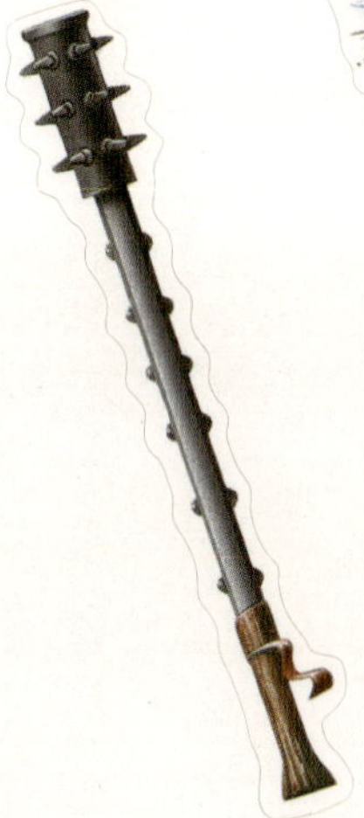

▲ Motte and bailey castle

▲ Fighting knights

Knights and castles

◄ Shield

► Warrior Knight

▲ Knight and lady

▲ Windsor Castle

► Longbow

▲ Banner

▲ Knight and warhorse

▲ Glamis Castle

▲ Shield

▲ Warrior Knight

▲ Knight and lady

▲ Windsor Castle

▲ Banner

▲ Longbow

▲ Knight and warhorse

▲ Glamis Castle

Cold castles

Medieval stone castles were cold, damp places with lots of draughts. A castle was not exactly a luxury home. Cold winds blew through the windows, which had no glass, and there was no central heating or running water. Wool hangings and tapestries on the walls, and rugs on the floors helped to keep rooms warm. Roaring fires burned in the huge fireplaces.

The lord of the castle and his family were the only people who slept in beds – most people slept on a wooden board covered in straw!

Workshops and other buildings were located inside the safety of the castle walls

The main entrance had a heavy barred gate called a portcullis and narrow slits for firing arrows to defend the castle

Design your own castle!

You will need:
• coloured pencils • paper • ruler

1. Imagine you have been asked to design a castle for your local lord! It is important that he can defend his castle and family against attacks by enemies.

2. Draw a detailed plan of your ideal castle, making sure it has plenty of defences. Colour in the different areas of use in the castle.

KEY:

1	Chapel	6	Main gate
2	Great hall	7	Guard room
3	Battlements	8	Kitchens
4	Prison tower	9	Stable
5	Portcullis	10	Royal tower

Knights and castles

▲ Knight of St John
Knights of this order lived like monks and followed very strict rules

▲ Knight in armour
This knight is wearing a protective helmet and patterned tunic

◄ Fighting Knights
Two brave knights battle against each other

▼ Motte and bailey castle
This was a wooden castle built on a hilltop and surrounded by a wooden fence

▲ Bodiam Castle
This moated castle is in southern England and it was built in the 1300s

◄ Mace
A club-shaped weapon used by knights in battle

▼ Horseback fight
Crusader and Saracen knights often fought on horseback

▲ Crossbow
Crossbows fired arrows powerfully and accurately, but they were slow to reload

KEY:

Knights

Castles

Weapons

Banners/Shields

◀ Glamis Castle

Located in Scotland, this castle is the scene for the play *Macbeth* written by William Shakespeare

▼ Longbow

A skilled longbow archer could shoot an arrow up to 300 metres

▲ Windsor Castle
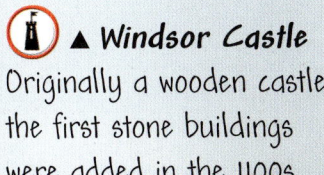

Originally a wooden castle, the first stone buildings were added in the 1100s

▲ Shield

Shields carried the colours and patterns of the knight's lord

▶ Warrior Knight

Knights wore armour to protect themselves in battle

▼ Knight and lady

Knights were taught to follow strict rules about how to behave towards women

▲ Knight and warhorse

Knights would normally have three horses - one for battle, one for riding and one for carrying loads

▲ Banner

Banners were carried by knights to show loyalty to their lord

**A crusader knight would share his tent with his beloved horse -
it must have been a bit of a squeeze!**

The biggest and best!

Read on to find out some amazing facts about knights and castles

■ Knights wore personal colours and symbols during battles and tournaments. These became known as coats of arms.

■ Young boys started to learn how to be a knight at about the age of seven, when they were sent to serve as a page in a castle.

■ Castles often had no bathroom for the servants. They had to wash in the local river or stream.

• Krak des Chevaliers in Syria is the biggest surviving Crusader castle. It was built on a hill of solid rock.

• The Bayeux Tapestry is an amazing 70 metres long. It shows the victory of William the Conqueror and his brave knights at the Battle of Hastings.

• The town of Carcassonne in southern France is rather like one huge castle. The whole town is surrounded by high walls, parts of which date back to AD600.

Q: What do you call a mosquito in a metal suit?
A: A bite in shining armour!

Discover more about brave knights and castle life

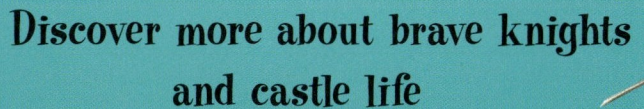

• The great hall was the centre of castle life. Large feasts of delicious food and wine were served as the lord and his guests were entertained by musicians, jesters, jugglers and acrobats.

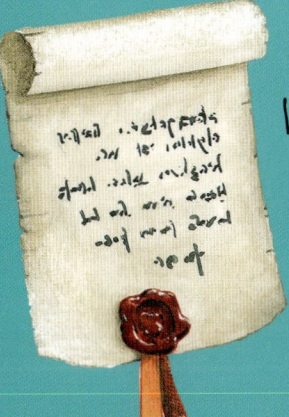

• A knight would write secret letters to the woman he loved. They would also write poems to each other expressing their feelings of love and devotion.

• The legend of St George tells how he killed a fierce dragon. George saved the people of Lydia (part of modern Turkey) from the fire-breathing dragon.

Knights had to behave according to a set of strict rules, known as the code of chivalry. This code involved being brave and honourable in battle and at tournaments.

A knight who did not follow the code of chivalry was disgraced and punished.

Medieval castles had no proper toilets! Instead, people sat on wooden seats over a long chute. The waste dropped down into the moat!

Q: Why did the ponytailed knight visit his doctor?
A: He was a little hoarse!

Fun facts

🏰 Early knights wore a type of armour called chainmail. It was made of thousands of tiny iron rings joined together.

🏰 Messengers called heralds carried messages between knights during battles.

🏰 Japanese warrior knights in the Middles Ages were known as samurai. A long curving sword was a samurai's most treasured possession.

Test your memory!

How much can you remember from your knights and castles sticker activity book? Find out below!

1. Which knight saved the people of Lydia by killing a fierce dragon?
2. Name the code which knights had to follow?
3. Which famous battle is featured on the Bayeux Tapestry?
4. Who started the building of Windsor Castle?
5. Did a knight's warhorse need to be small and lively or large and aggressive?
6. What was the name of the men who carried messages between knights during battles?
7. What name was given to Japanese warrior knights in the Middle Ages?
8. Is Beaumaris Castle in England, Scotland or Wales?
9. What room was the centre of castle life?
10. What was chainmail armour made from?

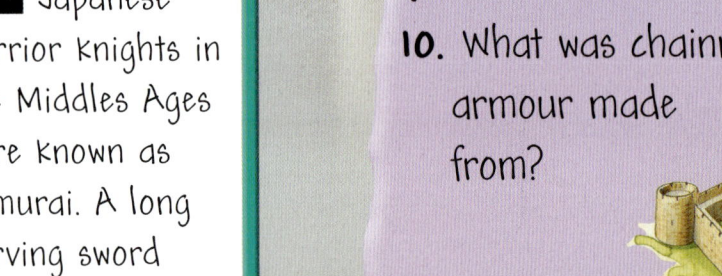

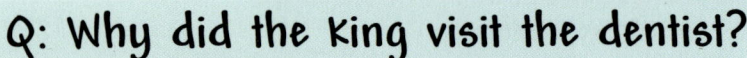

Q: Why did the King visit the dentist?
A: To get his teeth crowned!

11. Who started the building of Neuschwanstein Castle?

12. Which castle is the scene for the play *Macbeth*?

13. How many metres could a skilled longbow archer shoot an arrow?

14. Which weapon was faster to reload: a crossbow or a longbow?

15. In what country is the Krak des Chevaliers Castle?

16. Name the massive rock-hurling weapon used to attack castles.

17. What was Windsor Castle orginally made from?

18. Which castle is said to be haunted by the ghost of Edward II?

19. Is a motte and bailey castle on a hilltop or in a dip?

20. What is a mace?

Answers:

1. St George 2. Code of chivalry 3. Battle of Hastings
4. William the Conqueror 5. Large and aggressive
6. Messengers 7. Samurai 8. Wales 9. The great hall
10. Thousands of tiny iron rings joined together
11. King Ludwig of Bavaria 12. Glamis Castle
13. Up to 300 metres 14. Longbow 15. Syria
16. Trebuchet 17. Wood 18. Berkeley Castle
19. On a hilltop 20. A club-shaped weapon

English kings and queens have lived at Windsor Castle since William the Conqueror started building it over 900 years ago.

Beaumaris Castle in Wales, was the last castle built by Edward I of England. He was the greatest castle builder of his day.

A knight's warhorse needed to be large and aggressive. These brave horses would often bite and kick the enemy in battle.

Q: What did the knight give to his coughing horse?
A: Cough stirrup!

Other sticker books

You can now have even more fun and collect
all the sticker books in this series

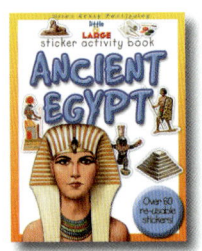
978-1-84236-660-8

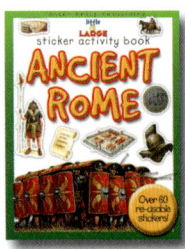
978-1-84236-661-5

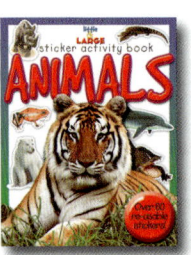
978-1-84236-303-4

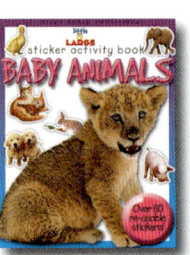
978-1-84236-244-0

978-1-84236-513-7

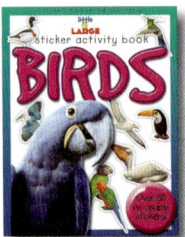
978-1-84236-304-1

978-1-84236-305-8

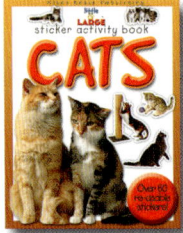
978-1-84236-662-2

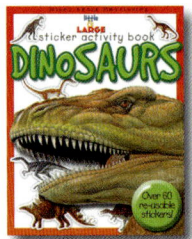
978-1-84236-302-7

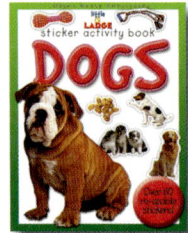
978-1-84236-663-9

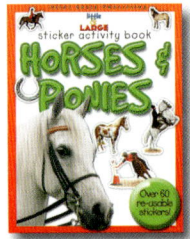
978-1-84236-514-4

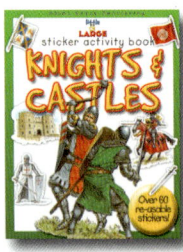
978-1-84236-255-6

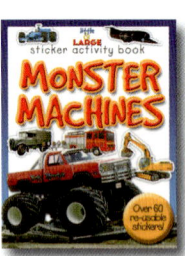
978-1-84236-671-4

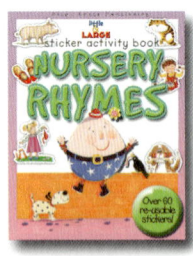
978-1-84236-246-4

978-1-84236-307-2

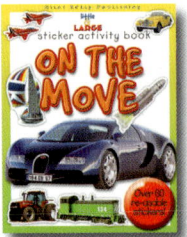
978-1-84236-245-7

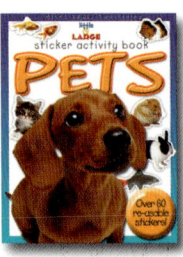
978-1-84236-306-5

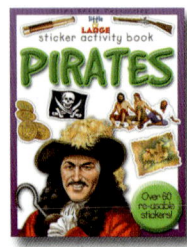
978-1-84236-669-1

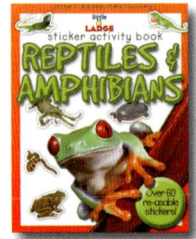
978-1-84236-254-9

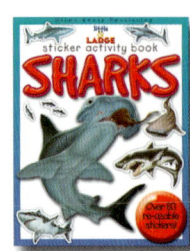
978-1-84236-512-0

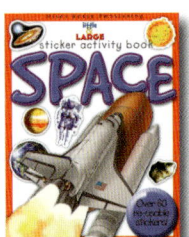
978-1-84236-247-1

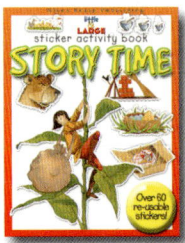
978-1-84236-515-1

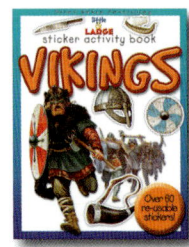
978-1-84236-668-4

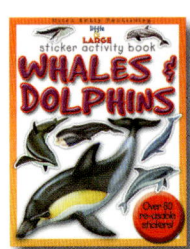
978-1-84236-672-1

978-1-84236-498-7